ISRAEL

Julie Murray

VISIT US AT

www.abdopublishing.com

Published by ABDO Publishing Company, PO Box 398166, Minneapolis, MN 55439.

Copyright © 2014 by Abdo Consulting Group, Inc. International copyrights reserved in all countries. No part of this book may be reproduced in any form without written permission from the publisher. Big Buddy Books™ is a trademark and logo of ABDO Publishing Company.

Printed in the United States of America, North Mankato, Minnesota.
032013
092013

 PRINTED ON RECYCLED PAPER

Coordinating Series Editor: Rochelle Baltzer
Editor: Sarah Tieck
Contributing Editors: Megan M. Gunderson, Marcia Zappa
Graphic Design: Adam Craven
Cover Photograph: *iStockphoto*: ©iStockphoto.com/maryTR.
Interior Photographs/Illustrations: *AP Photo*: AP Photo (p. 33), Yves Logghe (p. 29), Staff/Nightswander (p. 17), North Wind Picture Archives via AP Images (p. 31), Rex Features via AP Images (p. 19); *Getty Images*: Pictorial Parade/Hulton Archive (p. 16), Ahikam Seri/Bloomberg via Getty Images (p. 25); *Glow Images*: Elan Fleisher/LOOK-foto (p. 34), SuperStock (p. 13); *iStockphoto*: ©iStockphoto.com/earthmandala (pp. 21, 35); *Shutterstock*: Noam Armonn (p. 23), Paul_Brighton (p. 27), Yuriy Chertok (p. 25), Kobby Dagan (p. 35), fiphoto (p. 27), Globe Turner (pp. 19, 38), irisphoto1 (p. 11), Jelle vd Wolf (p. 9), Konstantnin (p. 38), liza1979 (p. 29), Mikhail Markovskiy (p. 15), Protasov AN (p. 37), Aleksandar Todorovic (p. 11), Nickolay Vinokurov (p. 21), wong yu liang (p. 34), Peter Zaharov (p. 35), Ron Zmiri (p. 5).

Country population and area figures taken from the CIA World Factbook.

Library of Congress Control Number: 2013932239

Cataloging-in-Publication Data

Murray, Julie.
Israel / Julie Murray.
   p. cm. -- (Explore the countries)
ISBN 978-1-61783-813-2 (lib. bdg.)
1. Israel--Juvenile literature. I. Title.
956--dc23
                                                                2013932239

Israel

Contents

Around the World

   Our world has many countries. Each country has different land. It also has its own rich history. And, the people have their own languages and ways of life.

   Israel is a country in Asia. What do you know about Israel? Let's learn more about this place and its story!

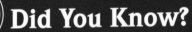

Did You Know?

Hebrew and Arabic are the official languages of Israel. English is also commonly spoken there.

Israel borders the Dead Sea. This is the saltiest natural lake in the world.

PASSPORT TO ISRAEL

Israel is located in a part of the world known as the Middle East. Lebanon, Syria, Jordan, and Egypt are its four bordering countries. The West Bank and the Gaza Strip are two bordering territories. The Mediterranean Sea forms the western border. The Gulf of Aqaba is to the south.

Israel is a small country. Its total area is 8,019 square miles (20,770 sq km). About 7.6 million people live there.

WHERE IN THE WORLD?

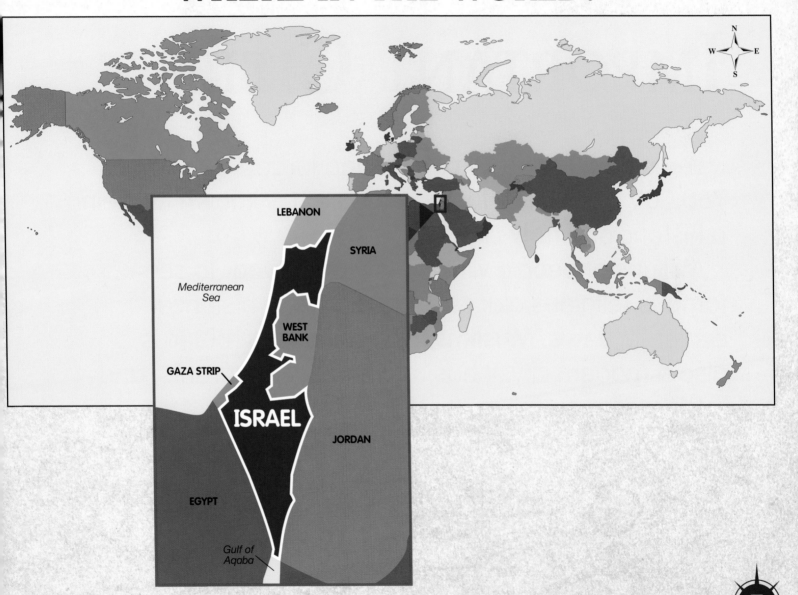

LEBANON

SYRIA

Mediterranean
Sea

WEST
BANK

GAZA STRIP

ISRAEL

JORDAN

EGYPT

Gulf of
Aqaba

IMPORTANT CITIES

Jerusalem is Israel's **capital** and largest city. About 760,000 people live there. Jerusalem is known for being a historic and **holy** city.

Millions of people visit this city every year to see famous religious places. Jerusalem is a historical center for **Jews**, **Muslims**, and **Christians**. But, it is also a modern city. It has museums, restaurants, and businesses.

SAY IT

Jerusalem
juh-ROO-suh-luhm

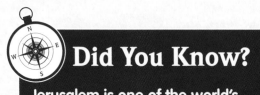

Did You Know?

Jerusalem is one of the world's oldest cities that people still live in.

The Western Wall is a famous place in Jerusalem. It is part of an ancient temple. Jews from around the world go there to pray.

Haifa

Tel Aviv

Jerusalem

ISRAEL

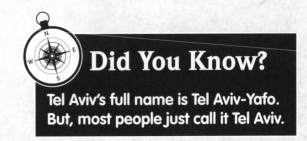

Did You Know?

Tel Aviv's full name is Tel Aviv-Yafo. But, most people just call it Tel Aviv.

Tel Aviv is Israel's second-largest city. It is home to about 400,000 people. This city is located on the Mediterranean Sea. It is known as a center of business in Israel.

Haifa is the third-largest city, with about 260,000 people. It lies on Mount Carmel. The city is located on a bay in the Mediterranean Sea. It is an important port.

SAY IT
Tel Aviv
tehl-uh-VEEV
Haifa
HEYE-fuh

Haifa is known for its beaches. Many cruise ships stop there.

Tel Aviv has popular restaurants, shops, and beaches. It is one of the most modern cities in the Middle East.

ISRAEL IN HISTORY

The first people settled in what is now Israel about 4,000 years ago. Hebrew, or **Jewish**, people began to settle the area in about 1500 BC. Soon, it became known as the Kingdom of Israel. Stories about this time are in the Bible.

King David and his son King Solomon made the Kingdom of Israel very strong. When Solomon died, the kingdom broke apart. Over the next centuries, many people fought to control this land. The Romans called it Palaestina, or Palestine.

King David was one of Israel's kings. There are many religious stories about him. He was a skilled fighter and he wrote verses that are in the Bible.

In the 600s, **Muslim** Arabs took over Palestine. Muslim powers ruled the area for many years. In the late 1800s, **Jews** wanted to take back part of Palestine from them.

In 1948, part of Palestine became Israel. It was meant as a homeland for Jews from around the world. But, Arabs in Palestine and nearby countries fought for this land. Today, many people are still working for peace in the area.

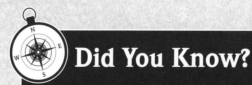

Did You Know?

The Gaza Strip and the West Bank are parts of Palestine that didn't become Israel. Today, these areas are territories.

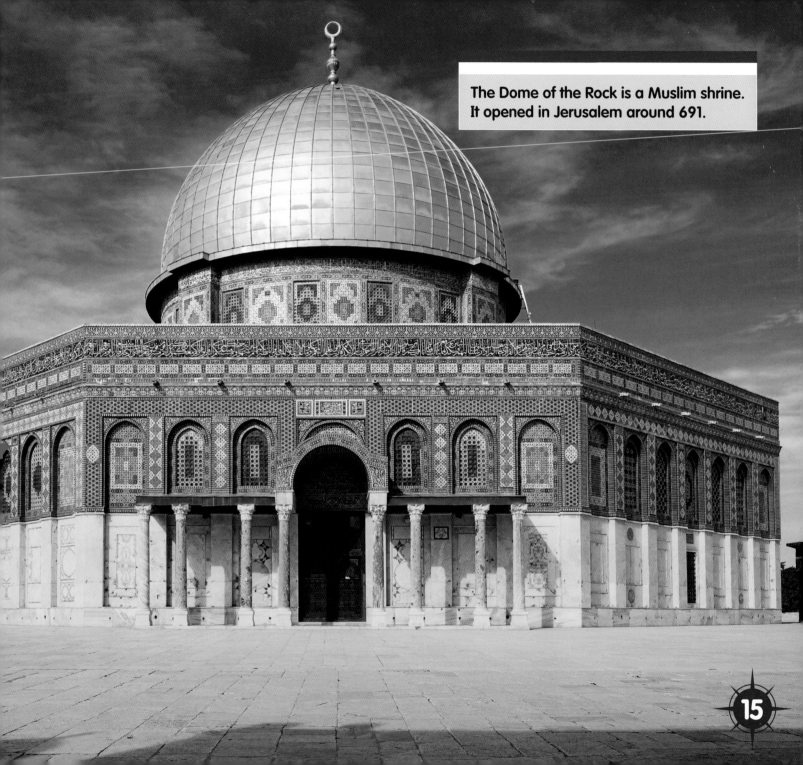

The Dome of the Rock is a Muslim shrine. It opened in Jerusalem around 691.

Timeline

1949

The Ghetto Fighters' House was founded in Israel. This important museum is about the **Holocaust**.

1948

On May 14, **Jews** proclaimed the State of Israel. The next day, five Arab countries attacked Israel. Israel won the fight and gained land.

1966

Israeli writer Shmuel Yosef Agnon won the Nobel Prize for Literature. This is a big honor.

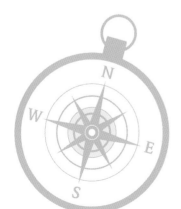

1994

Israel made a peace agreement with the country of Jordan. This ended a long history of fighting between them.

2012

Israel and the Gaza Strip exchanged rocket fire. People continued struggling for peace.

2010

A major forest fire destroyed areas of northern Israel.

AN IMPORTANT SYMBOL

Israel's flag was adopted in 1948. It has a blue Star of David on a white background. There are blue stripes above and below the star.

Israel's government is a **parliamentary democracy**. The prime minister is the head of government. The president is the head of state. The country's laws are made by a group called the Knesset.

Israel's flag colors are the same as a *tallit*, or Jewish prayer shawl. The Star of David is a Jewish symbol.

Benjamin Netanyahu became the prime minister of Israel in 2009.

ACROSS THE LAND

Israel has plains, mountains, valleys, coasts, and deserts. Most of the country's farms, people, and businesses are on a coastal plain near the Mediterranean Sea.

Mountain ranges are found in the Galilee region in the north. In the south is the Negev desert area. Major bodies of water include the Jordan River, the Sea of Galilee, and the Dead Sea.

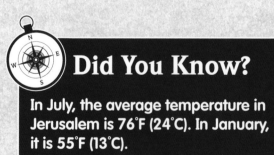

Did You Know?

In July, the average temperature in Jerusalem is 76°F (24°C). In January, it is 55°F (13°C).

The Dead Sea is the lowest area on Earth. It is in the Rift Valley in eastern Israel. The Dead Sea is saltier than the ocean!

The Jordan River flows into the Dead Sea. It forms part of Israel's eastern border.

Many types of animals make their homes in Israel. These include wolves, badgers, and hyenas. Scorpions and locusts are also found there.

People often think of Israel as a desert. But, it has varied land. So, many different types of plants grow there. They include olive trees, tulips, acacia trees, and grasses.

Olive trees are grown for their fruit. It is often made into olive oil.

23

Earning a Living

Israel has many important businesses. Some are privately owned. Others are owned by the government. Most Israelis have service jobs. They work for the government or help visitors. Others work in manufacturing.

Israel has some natural **resources**. Copper and clay come from its mines. Farmers produce tomatoes, citrus fruits, and potatoes. They also raise livestock such as sheep.

Did You Know?

Israel gets little rain much of the year. So, water from the Jordan River and the Sea of Galilee is used for farms.

Israel is known for manufacturing science-based products. These include medicines (*left*) and electronics.

Beef and dairy cattle are raised on Israel's farms.

LIFE IN ISRAEL

Israel is known for its long history and desert land. People often think of religious stories or camels and **Bedouins**. But today, Israel is a modern country.

Israelis eat foods such as hummus, falafel, and shawarma. Za'atar, mint, and garlic are popular spices. Some people follow religious diets or ways of eating.

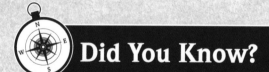

Did You Know?

In Israel, children must attend school between the ages of about 5 and 16. There are religious and non-religious schools.

Shawarma is a wrap filled with shaved meats, such as lamb or chicken.

Falafel is made of spiced vegetables such as chickpeas. They are formed into balls and then fried.

Most Israelis are **Jews**. Many follow Judaism. They observe holidays such as Rosh Hashanah. Each Friday, many honor the Sabbath with a special meal.

Some Israelis are Arabs. Most of them follow **Islam**. They observe the **holy** month of Ramadan and the holiday Id al-Fitr.

Sports are very popular in Israel. Soccer is one favorite. People there also enjoy tennis and basketball.

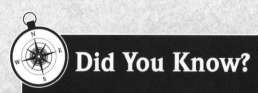

Did You Know?

The Sabbath is a day of rest and worship. In Judaism, it lasts from Friday evening to Saturday evening.

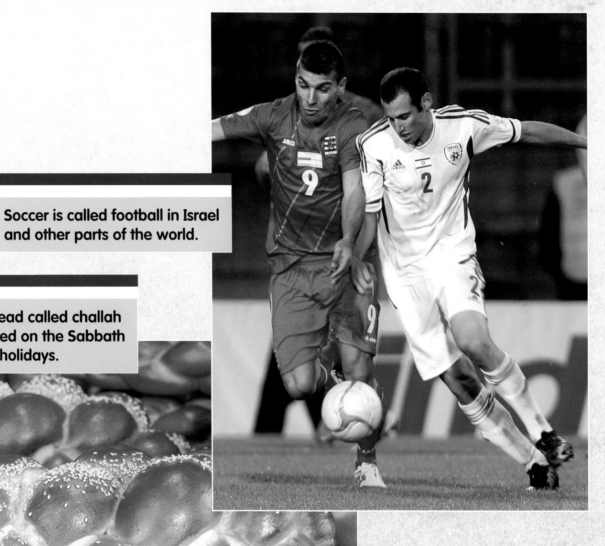

Soccer is called football in Israel and other parts of the world.

A type of bread called challah is often served on the Sabbath and Jewish holidays.

FAMOUS FACES

King Solomon lived in what is now Israel in the 900s BC. His father was King David. King David helped make the Kingdom of Israel powerful by taking over nearby land. Solomon ruled this large kingdom after King David.

King Solomon was also powerful. He built a temple and a palace in Jerusalem. He ruled until his death. Stories about King Solomon are in the Bible.

King Solomon was known as a wise man. So, other leaders such as the Queen of Sheba came to seek his advice.

Golda Meir was born in Kiev, present-day Ukraine, in 1898. In 1921, she joined a group that lived on a farm in Palestine. She belonged to a movement called Zionism. It supported creating a **Jewish** state in Palestine. In 1948, Meir became one of the founders of Israel.

Meir began working for the Israeli government. She was the prime minister from 1969 to 1974. During this time, there was fighting between Israel and Arab countries. Meir worked to strengthen Israel and create peace until her death in 1978.

SAY IT
Meir
may-IHR

Meir was known for being honest and tough.

Tour Book

Have you ever been to Israel? If you visit the country, here are some places to go and things to do!

 ## See

Visit the Dome of the Rock in Jerusalem. This is an important religious place for Muslims.

 ## Explore

Visit the White City of Tel Aviv. This large group of light-colored modern buildings was built between the 1930s and 1950s.

Remember

See Masada National Park. It overlooks the Dead Sea and has buildings that are about 2,000 years old! Take a hike or ride a cable car to the top.

Discover

Climb the steps of the Baha'i shrine and gardens in Haifa.

 Play

Spend time at the Sea of Galilee. It is also called Lake Tiberias. Many people vacation there.

A GREAT COUNTRY

The story of Israel is important to our world. The people and places that make up this country offer something special. They help make the world a more beautiful, interesting place.

Mount Zion is a historic place in Jerusalem. Many Bible stories take place there.

37

Israel Up Close

Official Name: State of Israel

Flag:

Population (rank): 7,590,758
(July 2012 est.)
(97th most-populated country)

Total Area (rank): 8,019 square miles
(154th largest country)

Capital: Jerusalem

Official Languages: Hebrew, Arabic

Currency: New Israeli shekel

Form of Government: Parliamentary
democracy

National Anthem: "Hatikva"
(The Hope)

Important Words

Bedouin (BEH-duh-wuhn) a member of an Arab tribe whose people live in Middle Eastern deserts. Bedouins live in tents and move often.

capital a city where government leaders meet.

Christian (KRIHS-chuhn) a person who practices Christianity, which is a religion that follows the teachings of Jesus Christ.

Holocaust the mass murder of Jews by the Nazis of Germany between 1941 and 1945.

holy important to a religion.

Islam a religion based on a belief in Allah as God and Muhammad as his prophet. Muslims are people who practice Islam.

Judaism (JOO-dee-ih-zuhm) a religion based on laws recorded in the Torah. A Jew is someone who practices Judaism or is related to the ancient Hebrews.

parliamentary democracy a government in which the power is held by the people, who exercise it by voting. It is run by a cabinet whose members belong to the legislature.

resource a supply of something useful or valued.

Web Sites

To learn more about Israel, visit ABDO Publishing Company online. Web sites about Israel are featured on our Book Links page. These links are routinely monitored and updated to provide the most current information available.

www.abdopublishing.com

Index